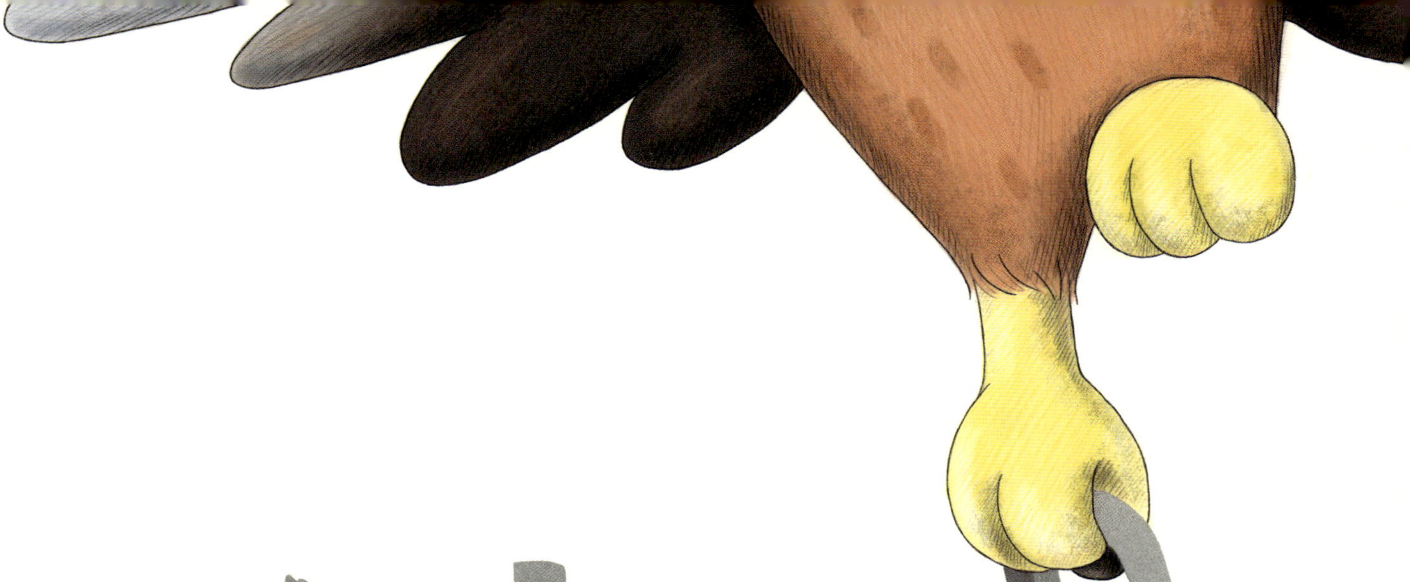

# WEIRDO GOES WILD

To our godson, Dash – Z.S. & N.L.

For my dad, Gareth
And my weirdo, Joel – M.F.

Dad

Likes: Camping, explaining things

Dislikes: Searching for missing cats

Mum

Likes: Music, talking to neighbours

Dislikes: Mess

Dora

Likes: Fancy things

Dislikes: Ordinary things

Bob

Likes: Screens, sleeping

Dislikes: People ignoring the schedule

PUFFIN BOOKS

UK | USA | Canada | Ireland | Australia | India | New Zealand | South Africa

Puffin Books is part of the Penguin Random House group of companies whose addresses can be found at global.penguinrandomhouse.com.

www.penguin.co.uk
www.puffin.co.uk
www.ladybird.co.uk

Penguin Random House UK

First published 2024

001



Printed in China

The authorized representative in the EEA is Penguin Random House Ireland, Morrison Chambers, 32 Nassau Street, Dublin D02 YH68

A CIP catalogue record for this book is available from the British Library

ISBN: 978-0-241-62375-6

All correspondence to:
Puffin Books, Penguin Random House Children's
One Embassy Gardens, 8 Viaduct Gardens, London SW11 7BW

FSC www.fsc.org MIX Paper | Supporting responsible forestry FSC® C018179

ZADIE SMITH NICK LAIRD

# WEIRDO GOES WILD

illustrated by
MAGENTA FOX

Maud

Likes: Kit, Judo, and being a bit weird
Dislikes: Vets, being teased

Kit

Likes: Pets, adventures
Dislikes: Not being allowed more pets

Derrick

Likes: Staying indoors, eating
Dislikes: Being alone

PUFFIN

Kit was going away.

*But where is she going?*
Derrick wanted to know.

Derrick never went away.
He liked the indoors.

Even if someone left
the window open,
he wasn't tempted.

*I've never slept in a forest,* said Kit. She was a bit nervous. She remembered that time Dora stayed out all weekend. Everyone had been so worried.

But eventually, Dora turned up in Mrs Mackenzie's wardrobe.

*Well, the school has sent a Kit List,* explained Mum. *There's nothing to worry about. You'll be in the Great Outdoors!*

*But there's <u>nothing</u> great about the outdoors!* cried Bob. *It's dark! It's full of wild animals! There's no telly!* Even if Bob had a Bob List, he wouldn't sleep in a forest.

Maud was worried. Who would Kit talk to if she couldn't get to sleep? Who would she hug if she got lonely?

*Will I be in a tent or in a room?* asked Kit.

*A tent,* said Mum. *But tents are really very nice these days. And there's going to be a bonfire!*

*Rather you than me, mate,* said Derrick.

*And what about the schedule?* Bob wanted to know.

On Tuesdays,
they did Judo.

On Wednesdays, they
had a Proper Rest.

On Thursdays, they
practised their
Signature Moves.

*It'll all be over before you know it,* said Dad.

Maud remembered this was what he'd said when the vet gave her that injection.

Kit got started on the Kit List. There was a lot of stuff to bring, but you had to put a label on each thing with your name written on it.

Bob was more worried about the things you couldn't bring:

*No Phones*

*No Tablets*

*No Laptops*

That was Bob's idea of a nightmare.

Maud checked the Kit List.

It didn't say NO MAUDS.

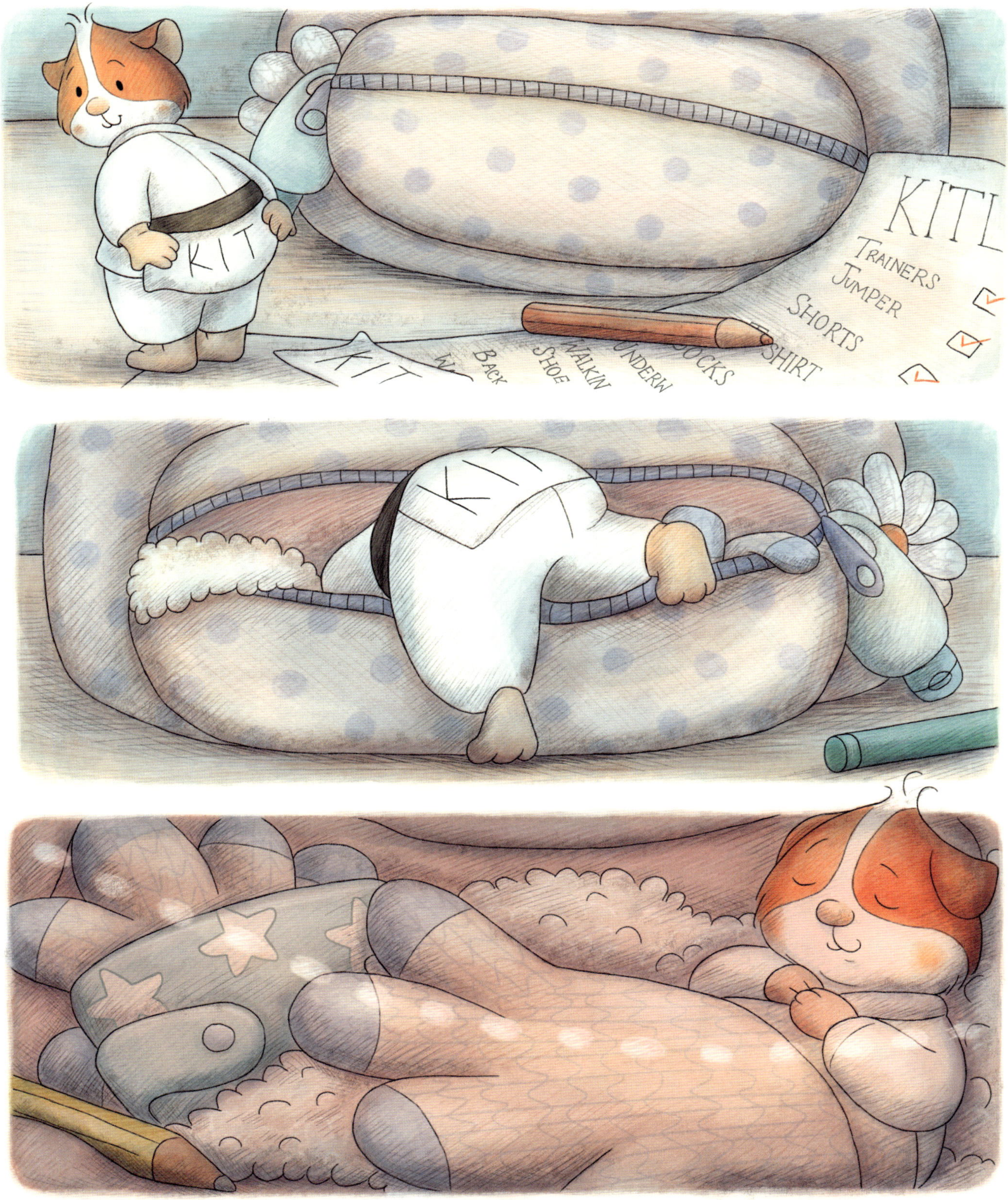

SCHOOL TRIP
SCHL 8US
CAMPSITE

When Maud woke up,
there was no sign of Kit.

And everything was different.

Instead of carpet, there was
leaves and mud and grass.

Instead of a ceiling, the wide-open sky.

Suddenly, Maud heard a rustling, and out of the bush rolled a strange round thing with a face in the middle.

*Hello,*
said Maud.

*Defence!*
shouted The Thing.

*What are you doing?*
asked Maud.

*Defending myself,*
said The Thing.

*Everyone in the forest has a defence,* said The Thing.
*This is 'The Hedgehog.' It's called that because I am one.*

*Have you got a defence strategy?*

*I have a signature move*, said Maud.

*Bend! Twist! Touch your toes!
It's called 'The Maud'.*

*It's a bit weird*,
said the hedgehog.
*And it could be spikier.*

*Oh, I am a bit of a weirdo*, said Maud
proudly. *But I am also a Maud.
And instead of spikes, I have judo.*

*Well, it's the spikes that make us hedgehogs the kings of the forest*,
said the hedgehog. *I mean, after the badgers. And the foxes.
And maybe the owls. We're definitely in the top four.*

The hedgehog was called Harvey, and he knew
everything about living in a forest.
He knew that rain brings the worms out.
He knew all the secret places squirrels hide their acorns.

He knew that soon it would be dark, and they were
going to need somewhere to camp for the night.

*This,* said Harvey, *is my natural habitat.*
*Watch and learn.*

*But the most important thing,* Harvey explained, *is to always be –*

ALERT!

Maud was worried.

Maybe she was going to go into the clouds.
Or up into forever overhead.

Then she remembered her Signature Move.

*You could always stay you know,* said Harvey.
*I've loads more to teach you.*
*Mud-chucking, stick-breaking, worm-slurping . . .*

Maud liked Harvey, but she had a schedule to get back to – not to mention Kit and the other animals.

*Well, then the most important thing,*
Harvey explained,
*is to make it seem like you were never here.*

Once everything was tidied up, it was time to go home.

But there were no maps in the Great Outdoors and No Phones.

How could you find your way? You had to follow your nose . . .

. . . and also the signs.

*This is* my *natural habitat,* said Maud.
*Watch and learn.*

Hedgehogs
Crossing

Back at home, Kit built a tent in her bedroom so all the animals could try it. And she brought popcorn! From the snack cupboard!

*But what do you do at night without telly?* Bob wanted to know.

*You tell stories,* explained Maud.

*And what do you lie on?* wondered Dora.

*Mostly leaves,* said Maud. *Some twigs.*

*What about snacks?* asked Derrick. There was no snack cupboard in the Great Outdoors.

*You just have to know all the secret places the squirrels hide their acorns,* said Maud.

*But the most important thing*
*is to always stay –*

ALERT!

*Oh, it's only Kit's mum*, said Derrick.
Kit's mum did *not* look happy.

Worrying about mess was
Kit's mum's Signature Move.

But there was
no need to panic.

Kit and Maud had learnt a lot
in the great outdoors.

*See?* said Kit.
*It's like we were never here!*

Secret places to hide popcorn to eat later:

1. In your shoe

2. Inside a book

3. In your pocket

4. Under your pillow